This book belongs to:

_____

_____

From:

_____

Scan for Reading
by Eleni Elefterias

To Eleftheria (Mali),
Jacinta, Mila and Terry.

Published by HELLENIC THEOREM PUBLISHERS.

© Text, characters and photographs copyright Eleni Elefterias-Kostakidis.

Eleni Elefterias
PO Box 513 Ashfield NSW 2131
elenielefterias.com.au
eleni@elenielefterias.com.au
hellenictheorem@gmail.com

First published 2023 by Hellenic Theorem Publishers.

The moral right of author and illustrator has been asserted.

Layout Design by Oliver Milgate.

All Rights Reserved. No part of this publication may be reproduced, stored in a retrieval system, or transmitted, in any form or in any means - by electronic, mechanical, photocopying, recording or otherwise - without prior written permission.

ISBN: 978-0-6489128-8-0 (Paperback)

ΕΠΙΣΚΕΨΗ ΣΤΟ ΠΑΝΑΘΗΝΑΪΚΟ ΣΤΑΔΙΟ

Visit to the Panathinaiko Stadium

by Eleni Elefterias

Another book from the Hellenic Theorem Series

Με λένε Ελευθερία και
Me LE-ne E-lef-the-RI-a ke

μένω στο Σίδνεϋ, στην
ME-no sto SYTH-ney stin

Αυστραλία.
Af-stra-LI-a

(My name is Eleftheria and I live in Sydney, in Australia.)

Φέτος πήγα στην Ελλάδα
Fe-tos PI-gha stin E-ll-A-da

για πρώτη φορά με τη
ghia PRO-ti fo-RA me ti

γιαγιά μου την Ελένη.
yia-YIA moo tin E-LE-ni.

(This year I went to Greece for the first time with my grandmother, Eleni.)

Στην Αθήνα, η γιαγιά με
Stin A-THI-na i yia-YIA me

πήγε στο Παναθηναϊκό
PI-ghe sto Pa-na-thi-na-i-KO

στάδιο.
STA-thi-o.

(In Athens my grandma took me to the Panathinaiko Stadium.)

Το λένε και Καλλιμάρμαρο,
To LE-ne ke Ka-li-MAR-ma-ro

(They call it the kalimarmaro,)

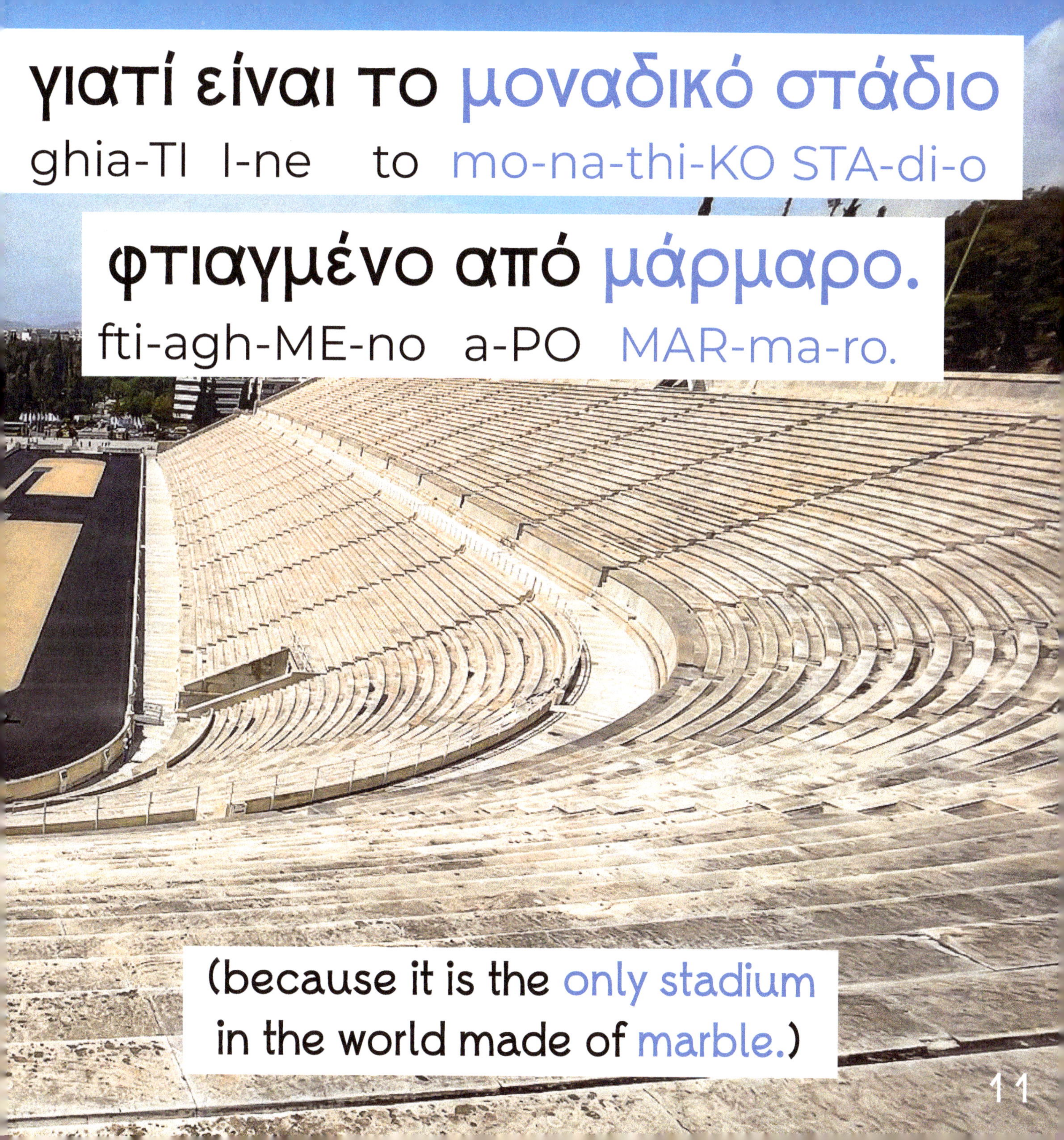

γιατί είναι το μοναδικό στάδιο
ghia-TI I-ne to mo-na-thi-KO STA-di-o

φτιαγμένο από μάρμαρο.
fti-agh-ME-no a-PO MAR-ma-ro.

(because it is the only stadium
in the world made of marble.)

Οι Αθηναίοι το
I A-thi-NE-oi to

χρησιμοποιούσαν για αγώνες
hri-si-mo-pi-OU-san ghia a-GHO-nes

από τα αρχαία χρόνια.
a-PO ta ar-HAI-a CHRO-ni-a.

(The Athenians used it for sports competitions from ancient times.)

Το 144μ.Χ το έφταιξαν από
To   144   to   EF-ti-a-xan   a-PO
πεντελικό μάρμαρο.
pen-tel-i-KO   MAR-ma-ro.

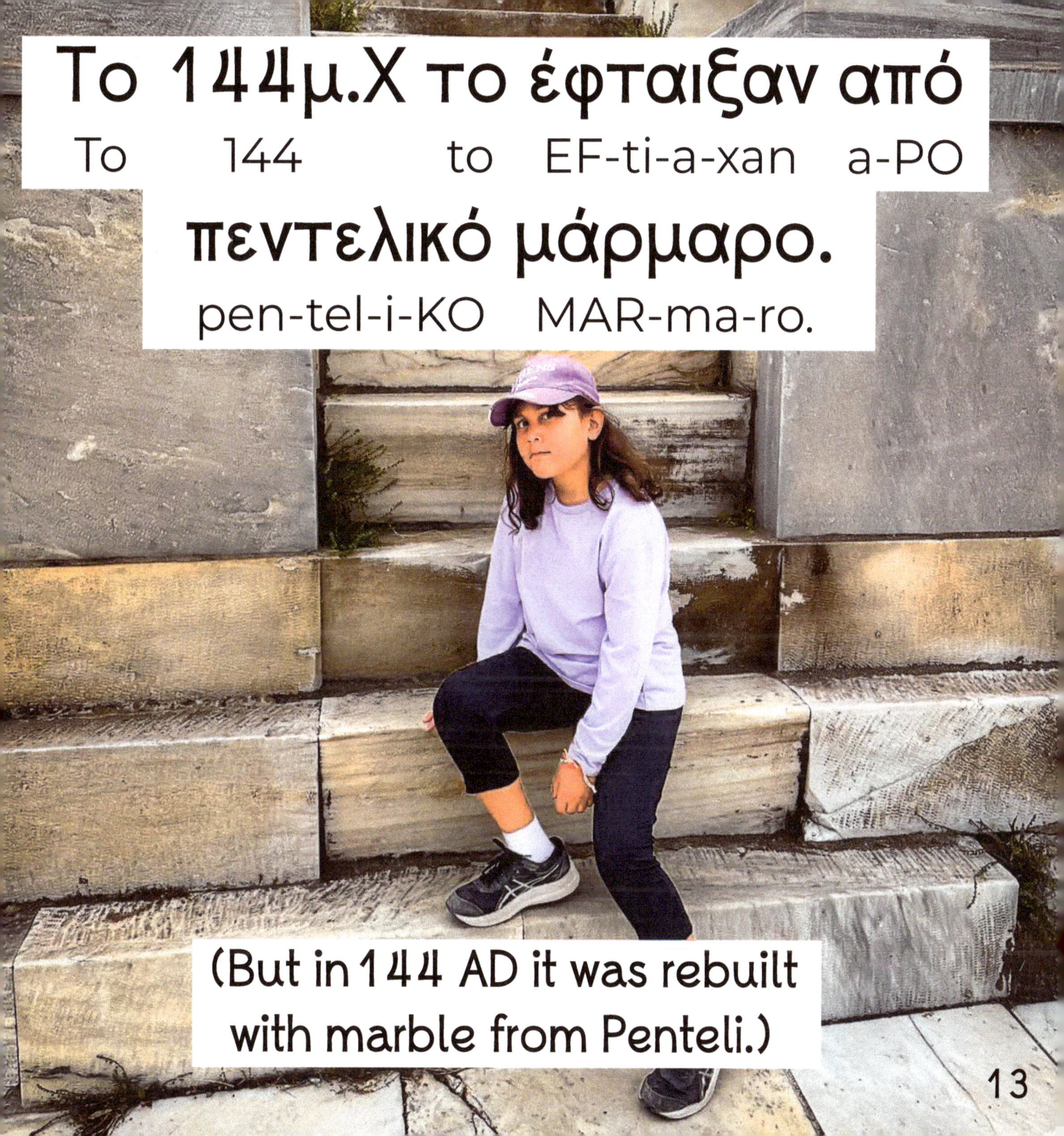

(But in 144 AD it was rebuilt with marble from Penteli.)

Στα μαρμάρινα καθίσματα
Sta   mar-MA-ri-na   ka-THIS-ma-ta

χωράνε 80,000 θεατές.
ho-RA-ne   80,000   the-a-TES.

(80,000 spectators can fit
in its marble seats.)

Στο στάδιο αυτό έγιναν οι
Sto   STA-thi-o af-TO E-ghi-nan i

πρώτοι μοντέρνοι Ολυμπιακοί
PRO-ti   mo-DER-ni   O-lym-pi-a-KI

Αγώνες το 1896.
a-GHO-nes   to   1896.

(In this stadium is where the first Modern Olympic Games took place in 1896.)

776 πΧ — 1894 μΧ

ΟΛΥΜΠΙΑΔΕΣ

Α	ΑΘΗΝΑΙ	1896
Β	ΠΑΡΙΣΙΟΙ	1900
Γ	ΑΓ. ΛΟΥΔΟΒΙΚΟΣ	1904
Δ	ΛΟΝΔΙΝΟΝ	1908
Ε	ΣΤΟΚΧΟΛΜΗ	1912
Ϛ	ΔΕΝ ΕΤΕΛΕΣΘΗ	1916
Ζ	ΑΜΒΕΡΣΑ	1920
Η	ΠΑΡΙΣΙΟΙ	1924
Θ	ΑΜΣΤΕΡΔΑΜ	1928
Ι	ΛΟΣ ΑΝΤΖΕΛΕΣ	1932
ΙΑ	ΒΕΡΟΛΙΝΟΝ	1936
ΙΒ	ΔΕΝ ΕΤΕΛΕΣΘΗ	

Υπάρχουν πλακέτες που
I-PAR-hoon pla-KE-tes poo

γράφουν πού έχουν γίνει
GHRA-foon poo E-hoon GHI-ni

Ολυμπιακοί αγώνες από το
O-lym-pi-a-KI a-GHO-nes a-PO to

1896 μέχρι σήμερα.
1896   ME-hri   SI-me-ra.

(There are plaques with all the cities that have held Olympic games since 1896.)

Εδώ βρήκα και το Σίδνεϋ!
E-THO VRI-ka ke to SYTH-ney!

Εκεί έγιναν οι Ολυμπιακοί
E-KI E-ghi-nan i O-lym-pi-a-KI

αγώνες το 2000.
a-GHO-nes to 2000.

(I found Sydney here too! That's where the Olympics took place in 2000.)

ΟΛΥΜΠΙΑΔΕΣ

ΚΕ	ΒΑΡΚΕΛΩΝΗ	1992
ΚΣΤ	ΑΤΛΑΝΤΑ	1996
ΚΖ	ΣΙΔΝΕΥ	2000
ΚΗ	ΑΘΗΝΑ	2004
ΚΘ	ΠΕΚΙΝΟ	2008
Λ	ΛΟΝΔΙΝΟ	2012
ΛΑ	ΡΙΟ	2016
ΛΒ	ΤΟΚΥΟ	2020

Το 2004 έγιναν για δεύτερη
To 2004 E-ghi-nan ghia THEf-te-ri

φορά στην Αθήνα.
fo-RA stin A-THI-na.

(In 2004 they were held for
a second time in Athens.)

Έτρεξα κι εγώ σ'αυτό το
E-tre-ksa ki e-GHO saf-TO to

στάδιο όπου έχουν τρέξει
STA-thi-o o-POO E-hoon TRE-ksi

πολλοί άλλοι αθλητές.
pol-I   A-lli   a-thli-TES.

(I ran around the stadium where many athletes have run before.)

Κάθισα κι εγώ στα καθίσματα
KA-thi-sa ki e-GHO sta ka-THIS-ma-ta

οπού είχαν καθίσει θεατές
o-POO I-han ka-THI-si the-a-TES

πάνω από 2,000 χρόνια πριν.
PA-no a-PO 2,000 CHRO-ni-a prin.

(I sat on the seats where the audience sat over 2000 years ago.)

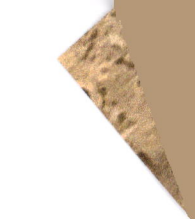

Μια μεγάλη μαρμάρινη
Mia me-GHA-li MAR-mar-in-i

πολυθρόνα λείπει γιατί
po-li-THRO-na LI-pi ghi-a-TI

βρίσκεται στο Μουσείο της
VRI-ske-te   sto   moo-SI-o   tis

Βρεττανίας!
Vre-ta-NI-as!

(One of the big marble armchairs is missing as it is in the British museum!)

Περπάτησα κι εγώ μέσα στην
Per-PA-ti-sa ki e-GHO ME-sa stin
υπόγεια στοά που την λένε και
i-PO-ghi-a sto-A poo tin LE-ne ke
'τρύπα της μοίρας',
TRI-pa tis MI-ras.

(I entered the underground tunnel known as the 'hole of fate',)

απ' όπου βγαίνουν οι αθλητές
ap-O-poo   VGHE-noon   i   a-thli-TES
για να αγωνιστούν.
ghi-a na a-gho-nis-TOON.

(from where the athletes emerged to compete.)

Στάθηκα πάνω στο βάθρο
STA-thi-ka   PA-no   sto   VA-thro

που στέκονται οι νικητές για
poo   STE-kon-te   i   ni-ki-TES ghi-a

να πάρουν τα μετάλλια της
na   PA-roon   ta   me-TA-li-a   tis

νίκης τους.
NI-kis   toos.

(I stood on the stand where the winning athletes stood to get their winning medals.)

Σήμερα γίνονται διάφορες
SI-me-ra GHI-non-te THIA-a-fo-res

εκδηλώσεις στο στάδιο,
ek-thi-LO-sis sto STA-thi-o

ακόμη και μουσικές
a-KO-mi ke moo-si-KES

συναυλίες.
si-nav-LI-es

(Today they hold various events in the stadium, including music concerts.)

Πολλοί τουρίστες το
Po-LI   too-RIS-tes   to

επισκέπτονται κάθε χρόνο.
e-pis-KEP-ton-te KA-the CHRO-no.

Είμαι πολύ τυχερή και
I-may po-LI   ti-HE-ri   ke

χαρούμενη που το
ha-ROO-me-ni poo   to

είδα από κοντά.
I-tha a-PO Kon-TA.

(Many tourists visit it every year. I am so lucky and glad I got see it firsthand.)

GREEKLISH GUIDE

Α α	άλφα	Alpha	fAther
Β β	βήτα	Vita	Vital
Γ γ	γάμμα	GHamma (Y as in yellow, YI as in year or GH, between game + yard)	Yes
Δ δ	δέλτα	THelta (Hard th)	Then
Ε ε	έψιλον	Epsilon	Egg
Ζ ζ	ζήτα	Zita	Zebra
Η η	ήτα	Ita	India, Era
Θ θ	θήτα	THita (Soft th)	THrone
Ι ι	ιώτα	Iota	India, Era
Κ κ	κάππα	Kappa	Kitchen
Λ λ	λάμδα	Lamtha	Lamb
Μ μ	μι	Mi	Mother

Ν ν	νι	Ni	Nice
Ξ ξ	ξι	KSi (Like x)	taXi
Ο ο	όμικρον	Omicron	hOt
Π π	πι	Pi	Peanut
Ρ ρ	ρω	Ro (rolled on the front of the tongue)	Rock
Σ σ ς	σίγμα	Sigma	Sand
Τ τ	ταύ	Tuf	Tennis
Υ υ	ύψιλον	Ipsilon	India
Φ φ	φι	Fi	Fine
Χ χ	χι	Hi	Hair, How
Ψ ψ	ψι	PSi	liPS
Ω ω	ωμέγα	Omegha	hOt

Note to parents and teachers

The book is meant to be read phonetically. For free audio examples, pronunciation guides and educational materials go to eleni@elenielefterias.com.au or YouTube & Tiktok: #elenielefterias.

Eleni Elefterias is an academic and teacher of Modern Greek who enjoys writing songs, lyrics and stories for children in Greek. She is the creator and writer of the HELLENIC THEOREM concept for which she is creating a bilingual series of fun educational books for children.

ACKNOWLEDGEMENTS

Thankyou to Dr Panayiota Nazou for help with copy editing of the Greek text.

PHOTO CREDITS:

Pg.23 - Dolya, S. (2014). The Lighting of the flame at the Panathinaiko Stadium for the Sochi Winter Olympics in Russia, 2014. [Photograph] Available at: https://sergeydolya.livejournal.com [Accessed 27 Nov. 2023].

Pg.28 - Peric, S. (2018). The Panathenaic Stadium or Kallimarmaro. [Photograph] Shutterstock. Available at: https://www.shutterstock.com/image-photo/athens-greece-april-17-2018-panathenaic-1718893522 [Accessed 27 Nov. 2023].

Pg.34 - Stefanos, Pantouvaki, S. and Greek National Opera (2014). Zorba, the Greek. [Photograph] Available at: https://sofiapantouvaki.com/ballet/ [Accessed 27 Nov. 2023].

All other photos by Eleni Elefterias and William Kostakidis.

www.ingramcontent.com/pod-product-compliance
Lightning Source LLC
Chambersburg PA
CBHW061800290426
44109CB00030B/2908